CW01085482

# GREEK

# MYTHOLOGY

Disclaimer: All attempts have been made by the author to provide
factual and accurate content. No responsibility will be taken by the
author or publisher for any damages caused by misuse of the content described in this book. The content of this book has been de-
rived from various sources. A pen name may have been used to
protect the privacy of the author. Please consult an expert before
attempting anything described in this book.

Hill Tech Ventures Inc.
Publishing Division | Nanaimo, Canada
Printed in the United States

# GREEK

# MYTHOLOGY

*Discover the Ancient Secrets of*

*Greek Mythology*

MARTIN R. PHILLIPS

## ABOUT THE AUTHOR

# MARTIN R. PHILLIPS

 Martin R. Phillips is an extremely passionate historian, archaeologist, and most recently a writer. Ever since Martin was a young boy he has been fascinated with ancient cultures and civilizations.

In 1990, Martin graduated with distinction from the University of Cambridge with a double major in History and Archaeology. Upon graduation, Martin worked as an archeologist and travelled the world working in various excavation sites. Over the years, while working as an archaeologist, Martin became very well cultured and gained great insights into some of the most historic civilizations to ever exist. This first hand insight into the ancient cultures of the world is what sparked Martin's newest passion, history writing and story telling.

In 2012, Martin decided to retire from archeology to focus on writing. Over the years he has seen and experienced a great deal of fascinating things from all over world. Martin now spends the majority of his free time putting all of his research, experience, and thoughts onto paper in an attempt to share his knowledge of the ancient cultures with the world.

Over the past few years Martin has excelled in his writings. His narrative style has a way of combining the cold hard facts with a story teller's intrigue which makes for an excellent reading experience.

"Live your life to the fullest and enjoy the journey!"

*- Martin R. Phillips*

# TABLE OF CONTENTS

# INTRODUCTION

One of the most interesting aspects of the ancient Greeks is their mythology. Although only a small handful of people still believe the myths to be true, what remains is that Greek mythology fascinates us in a way that is almost incomparable to other ancient systems of belief.

Culture has yet to turn away from the mythology of the ancient Greeks, and this fact can be seen in various aspects of our modern life. Through various forms of entertainment, we come across themes and events depicted in Homer's works of the Iliad and Odyssey. We find ourselves viewing and referencing the strength and trials of Heracles. We even find various parallels between the lives and myths of the ancient Greeks to our own modern world.

The history of Greece herself cannot be separated by the mythology of its ancient peoples. From heroes such as Heracles and Perseus, to the underhanded dealings of gods and mortals alike, their story is one a creative attempt to understand the forces which dwell about us and within us.

In this book you will find specific stories central to Greek mythology. This is a key into understanding the mindset, not only of these ancient peoples, but of our modern world as well. We may not subscribe as the Greeks did to these myths as factual accounts of historical events, however, these tales allegorically represent the things that humankind still endures and rejoices in.

In this text, you will find the spirit of love, of nature, of war and of peace. These myths often deal with very blunt subject matter, as they were the dominant lens through which the world was viewed during much of ancient Greece.

The research and writing involved in bringing you this collection of Greek mythology has been an absolute pleasure, and I hope that you are as fascinated in reading this as I was in putting it together.

Thanks again, I hope you enjoy it!

# CHAPTER 1

*In the Beginning, There was Chaos*

In this chapter, we will be discussing the origin of the universe according to Greek mythology and the generations of the primordial gods, the Titans, and the Olympians.

According to Greek mythology, the universe began as an abyss. There was no matter, no light, no life or consciousness outside of this primordial chasm. Yet it was out of this very void, known as Chaos (or Khaos) that not only the Titans and later the gods of Olympus were sprung, but existence itself.

It was from Chaos that Gaia (or Gaea, "mother earth") was formed. Along with Gaia, Tartarus (the abyss, often described as a vast cave-like space beneath the earth, comparable to hell in Judeo-Christian belief), Eros (desire/biological imperative; some myths include him as a primordial god, while others claim him as a child of Aphrodite) Erebus (darkness) and Nyx (the night) were also spawned of Chaos. While other beings that would represent other necessary factors for life as we know it were later formed by Gaia and her ilk, the initial building blocks of reality were spawned directly from Chaos.

The Chaos mythos in ancient Greek religion is an interesting one. Although the myths were around long before them, two poets were the earliest sources of known, written accounts dealing with the religion of ancient Greece. Those two men were Homer and Hesiod.

Homer is best known for his two epics Iliad and Odyssey which deal largely with the Trojan wars; wars that up until more recently were considered to be a complete fabrication. It's not within the scope of this book to delve too deeply into the purported Trojan wars themselves outside of the later chapter regarding Homer's works; however, reference to these epics form much of the basis of our understanding of Greek mythological belief.

Hesiod is also best known for two epic poems, Theogony and Works and Days. It is with Theogony that this text is primarily concerned, as it delves into the mythological creation and formation of all that exists, along with the Olympian gods, their progenitors and progenies.

At the earliest times within the Greek creation myth, there was, as yet, no male presence. Gaia took it upon herself to rectify this by birthing Uranus. Gaia produced other children asexually, they were: Ourea (mountains) and Pontus (sea). Thus completes the basic structure of the planet as the Greeks would view it.

Gaia bore many other children however. With her son Uranus, she bore the Hecatonchires (indomitable giants with a hundred hands), the Titans (a powerful race of deities with whom the next chapter is primarily concerned), the Cyclopes (more commonly Cyclops; one-eyed giants) and Echidna (often known as the mother of all monsters).

With Tartarus, she conceived and gave birth to her final son Typhon. Typhon was a dragon with a hundred heads, considered the most deadly of all monsters, and in some traditions, considered the father of all monsters.

Other primordial gods produced their own offspring which covered much of life's experience. Erebus and Nyx generated Aether (the heavens, also the air which the gods breathed) and Hemera (day). On her own, Nyx generated many descendants. These were Apate (deception), Eris (discord), Geras (maturation, or aging), Hypnos (sleep), the Keres (eaters of the dead or wounded on the battlefield), the Moirai (the fates), Momus (blame or denunciation), Moros (doom), Nemesis (revenge or retribution), Oizys (suffering), Oneiroi (Dreams), Philotes (affection) and Thanatos (death).

Uranus also produced his own children, although this was not by choice. His children were purportedly spawned when Cronos {one of the principle Titans} castrated Uranus. The blood that had spilled would go on to create the Erinyes (the furies, female deities of vengeance), the Giants (aggressive and strong beings, although not necessarily larger than human), the Meliae (ash tree nymphs). Also, when the severed genitals of Uranus washed ashore, Aphrodite (the goddess of love among other things) came into being among the sea foam.

While there are many other gods in the Greek pantheon, the present list is intended to show the first few emanations of Greek deities from Chaos to Aphrodite. Other gods, their children, consorts, etc. will be referenced in later chapters.

It is interesting to note that while Greek mythology was unique in many ways, there are common threads throughout many of the world's religions. For instance, in the belief of Judaism and its descendants Christianity and Islam, at the time of creation, the world was without form and [was] void. The formation came through god's will. Although these religions are monotheistic (belief in one god) as opposed to the polytheistic (belief in multiple gods) religion of the ancient Greeks, the story of creation has its similarities. The primary difference being that where the Greeks saw many emanations of gods that created existence, in the monotheistic religion, this was carried out by one god alone.

Other religions with similarities are the Babylonian where the earth began as a dark, watery chaos; the Hindu cosmology, the universe began as empty and dark. Even Norse mythology has its origin story begin in chaos.

It is hardly difficult to realize that in order to have an account of creation, there has to be something before creation. Even the scientific theory of the big bang has the universe composed with all matter in an infinitely small point; outside of this was nothingness (which could be called chaos).

*Martin R. Phillips*

# CHAPTER 2

## The Titans' Rule

The story of the rise of the Titans begins with the god of the sky, Uranus. Uranus (the sky) and Gaia (the earth) were spouses, lovers and, together, parented the Hecatonchires, the Cyclopes, the Echidna and the Titans.

Uranus and Gaia's love affair was the stuff of legend (forgive the pun.) Uranus so loved Gaia that at night, he embraced her on all sides, mating with her. He was a devoted spouse, but was obsessed with power.

While Uranus was affectionate toward Gaia, and favored those that he would come to call Titans, he feared and despised the Hecatonchires, the Giants and the Cyclopes. He imprisoned them all in Tartarus, deep within Gaia.

The imprisonment of her children caused Gaia great pain emotionally and physically. In order to reap vengeance on her consort Uranus for what he had done to her and her children, Gaia fashioned a sickle made of flint and approached her Titan children for help. The plan was to castrate Uranus.

None of the Titans were willing to risk a confrontation with Uranus with the exception of the youngest and the most ambitious Titan. His name was Cronus.

Cronus took the sickle and laid in wait for his father to arrive. When Uranus came, Cronus ambushed him and succeeded in castrating him. Cronus cast the severed genitals into the sea, the blood of which would create the giants, the meliae and the erinyes. When the genitals washed up to shore, Aphrodite was created.

Uranus cursed his children and called them Titanes theoi, or "straining gods." There are differing legends on what happened to the sickle at this point. Some claimed that the sickle was buried in Sicily. Others would claim that the sickle had been cast into the sea. One Greek historian claimed to have found the sickle at Corcyra.

With Uranus out of the picture as ruler, Cronus came to power. Although his mother Gaia had intended for her other children, the Cyclopes and the hundred-handed ones to be released from their captivity, Cronus left them prisoners inside Tartarus. Along with them, he also imprisoned the giants. Having now angered both of his parents, Gaia and Uranus prophesied that Cronus would be himself overthrown by one of his children.

Cronus had married his sister Rhea and, fearing the prophecy of the earth and the sky, he took upon himself a desperate plan to preserve his power. When Rhea began to bear children, Cronus immediately devoured them. Although his children were immortal like him, they would, in their turn, be imprisoned within his belly.

Each of his children, the first of those who would come to be the gods of Olympus, were devoured by Cronus in this manner with the exception of the youngest child. Rhea was fed up with Cronus's actions and when she was about to bear her sixth and final child, she hid away and, once her child was born, she hid him in a cave on Mount Ida in Crete. This child's name was Zeus.

Knowing that Cronus would insist upon devouring the child, Rhea took a stone and wrapped it in swaddling clothes. Cronus devoured the stone, thinking it to be his child.

Despite Cronus's treatment of his children, the time during the rule of Cronus and Rhea was referred to as The Golden Age of the Gods. The earth was devoid of immorality. The inhabitants of the earth were moral on their own, and so did not require laws to keep them in line. This was before the existence of humankind.

There are different myths as to how Zeus was raised. One has him being raised by Gaia herself. Another has him being raised by a nymph named Adamanthea who, in order to protect the child, suspended him from a tree between the sky, the sea, and the earth, therefore keeping him just outside his father's kingdom and therefore outside of his perception. Another myth has Zeus being raised by a shepherd family in exchange for the protection of their flocks. In another telling, he was raised by a different nymph named Cynosura. In this myth, Zeus's gratitude would lead him to place Cynosura among the stars.

Yet another, and one of the more popular myths of the time, has Zeus being raised by a goat. His cries are said to have been covered by a group of armored dancers who would bang their shields together, shout and clap in order to mask the child's cries, thus keeping him outside the knowledge of Cronus.

Regardless the differing myths associated with his infancy, Zeus grew to become very powerful. When he reached manhood, he was set on overthrowing his father Cronus, and releasing his siblings from within the ruler's body. He met with Metis, a Titan of deep knowledge and wisdom. She gave him an emetic (a substance which causes one to purge) potion to give to his father.

According to one myth, Zeus slipped the concoction into Cronus's nightly drink of mead. Upon drinking the mixture, Cronus began to grow violently ill. He first vomited up the stone which he had thought to be Zeus, and then the children whom he had eaten. These children of Cronus and Rhea were quick to ally themselves with Zeus. They were Demeter, Hades, Hera, Hestia and Poseidon.

What followed is often referred to as the Titanomachy or War of the Titans. This conflict between the Titans on Mount Othrys, and the children of Cronus from Mount Olympus would last for ten years. Zeus, in search of more allies against the Titans travelled deep into Gaia to Tartarus and freed the Hecatonchires, the Giants and the Cyclopes. In gratitude for their release, the Cyclopes forged thunder and lightning and gave them to Zeus.

The Olympians would face nearly all of the Titans in this war with the exception of Themis and her son Prometheus; these two allied themselves with Zeus.

With his new allies and powers, the Olympians would defeat the Titans. Upon victory, Zeus imprisoned the Titans in Tartarus as Uranus and Cronus had imprisoned the Hecatonchires and the Cyclopes.

Zeus forced Atlas, one of the leaders of the Titan army, to hold up Uranus at the western edge of Gaia by his shoulders in order to prevent the mating of the two, and the possibility of further Titan births. It's commonly thought that Atlas was forced to hold up the earth, and is often pictured as supporting the globe on his back. However, this is a more modern interpretation, and the actual myth was that of separating Uranus and Gaia.

The Titan rule had come to an end, and the rule of Olympus had started.

# CHAPTER 3

*The Olympian Rule*

Although which gods are included in the list of twelve Olympians varies, this number would be a constant of the major inhabitants of Olympus. Here it becomes useful to give an account of the major Olympian gods, their importance and their attributions. As the various consorts of these deities could fill up a book on their own, they will only be referenced in cases of particular importance.

Aphrodite was, as stated above, born from the sea foam after Cronus's genitals were cast into the sea. She was the goddess of love and beauty. She was among the gods invited to the wedding of Peleus and Thetis who would become the parents of the legendary Achilles. It was said that the only goddess not to be invited to the wedding was Eris, the goddess of discord.

When Eris showed up anyway, true to her nature, she tossed a golden apple into the center of the other goddesses inscribed with the words, "to the fairest."

Three of the goddesses immediately claimed that the gift was theirs by right of their beauty. These were Aphrodite, Hera and Athena.

When the three could not come to a decision regarding ownership of the golden apple, each thinking themselves to be the fairest of the goddesses, they brought the matter before Zeus. Wanting to avoid the quarrel, Zeus passed the decision onto Paris of Troy.

Paris was the son of the Trojan King Priam. The goddesses washed themselves in the spring of Mount Ida and went before Paris for his decision. They rent their clothing and asked him to judge. Although having been given permission to set his own conditions by Zeus, he could not decide among them as he found them all to be supremely beautiful.

The goddesses, undaunted by his inability to decide between them began offering him various things in exchange for his declaration of who was the fairest. Athena offered him wisdom, courage, and glory in battle; Hera offered control of Europe and Asia; but it was Aphrodite whose offer he accepted. Her offer was to grant him a wife who was more beautiful than all of the women of the earth.

The problem with Aphrodite's offer was that this woman was already married to a Spartan king named Menelaus. Undaunted, Paris abducted his new goddess-given bride, a woman named Helen out from under Menelaus. The legend goes that the other two goddesses, scorned Aphrodite and Paris for this, and they would go on to initiate the Trojan War, of which Homer's Iliad is largely concerned.

Apollo was the god of the sun, of light, of truth, and poetry among other things. He was often depicted as bearing a bow and arrow, or often a lyre. He was the son of Zeus and Leto, a daughter of Coeus and Phoebe (Titans), and twin brother to Artemis. Due to Hera's anger and jealousy of Leto as her husband had lain with her and the two produced offspring, Apollo's early life was largely occupied by protecting his mother against Hera's wrath.

Hera's first attempt on Leto was by sending Python, a dragon who dwelled beneath the living surface of Gaia. In order to be equipped to protect his mother, Apollo entreated Hephaestus to provide him with armaments. He received his iconic bow and arrow and, at only four days old, Apollo was said to have slain Python.

Hera wasn't done going after Leto, however. Her next attempt on Leto was commenced by sending the giant Tityos to dispatch her rival. Tityos was around twenty two square miles' worth of giant but, with the help of his sister Artemis, Tityos was defeated and cast into Tartarus by Zeus. While in Tartarus, Tityos was doomed to have his liver perpetually consumed by vultures.

Although he was considered a healer of man and god in Greek mythology, he also could bring death and disease with his arrows. One notable instance of this began with a simple insult.

Niobe was the wife of Amphion, one of the founders of Thebes and its ruler. She boasted to Leto that she had seven times as many children (seven sons and seven daughters) as Leto's two: Apollo and Artemis. Apollo and Artemis swiftly killed all (or in some versions, all but one) of Niobe's children; Apollo killed the sons while Artemis killed the daughters.

Apollo was bisexual and had a vast number of male and female consorts. He bore many children, however the story of Apollo and Daphne is one of the most famous. As the story goes, Apollo was remarking to Eros that his bow and arrow were above his station, that he was unfit to wield them.

Eros, having had enough of Apollo's taunts shot two arrows: A golden arrow of love through Apollo's heart and a leaden arrow of hate or disgust into the nymph Daphne. Apollo immediately pursued the nymph who was disgusted and fled his advances. She entreated her father Peneus, the river god to help her. Her father turned her into a laurel tree, but Apollo's love of her was unwavering. He embraced the branches, but even they shrank away from him. He declared that as he retained eternal youth, so should the leaves of the tree never decay. He would guard the tree from any who would do it harm, and use its branches as crowns for the leaders of the world.

Ares was the god of war. A son of Zeus and Hera (one of Zeus's rare dalliances with his own wife), Ares took his sister Enyo (goddess of destruction) as his consort. He was the father of Phobos (fear) and Deimos (terror) borne from Aphrodite. According to Homer, Ares was despised by his father Zeus for his lust for war.

While he was immortal, and loved nothing more than warfare, he was highly intolerant of pain. In Homer's Iliad, Ares was injured in the battlefield of Troy, and his cries were heard throughout the world. He went back to Olympus whining to his father Zeus to heal him. Zeus quickly let Ares know how much he was despised but, as Ares was his son, he did in fact heal him.

Ares is said to have always gone into war with Enyo joining him on his chariot, and this chariot was driven by Phobos and Deimos.

Artemis, twin of Apollo, was the goddess of the hunt, the moon, the forests and the hills. She was the first of the twins to be born, and actually acted as midwife to her mother Leto during Apollo's birth. Her weapon was, like that of her brother, the bow.

Artemis believed her destiny to be as a midwife, and unlike many of the philandering gods, she remained a virgin. All of her companions were also virgins and, one day as they were bathing, a man named Actaeon came upon them. He was hunting with his hounds at the time, but was struck by the beauty of Artemis and her cohorts and stopped to gaze upon them further.

When Artemis discovered the man peeping at herself and her companions, she became furious and turned him into a stag. His hunting dogs, no longer recognizing their master tore him to pieces.

Artemis was certainly not one to be trifled with. When Agamemnon, one of the legendary warriors of the Trojan War in Iliad, offended Artemis, she exacted her vengeance by calming the winds which bore Agamemnon's fleet toward Troy. Stranded in the middle of the sea, Agamemnon's only choice to appease Artemis was to offer up his daughter Iphigenia.

There are differing accounts as to what exactly happened when Artemis came upon Iphigenia. Some myths say that Artemis spared the woman because of her bravery, others say that Iphigenia was taken as a priestess to help worshippers offer sacrifice to the goddess, while still others say that Athena did in fact take Iphigenia as sacrifice.

Athena was the goddess of wisdom, intelligence, crafts, and architecture and was the patron goddess of Athens which bears her name. Athena's birth is as interesting as any other myths about her. She was borne of the goddess Metis.

Metis was the goddess of wisdom and craftiness. Zeus and Metis became entangled in a romantic tryst but, fearing a prophecy which stated that Zeus's offspring by Metis would come to be more powerful than Zeus himself, he consumed Metis (in some versions, he turned her into a fly first) as his father Cronus had done with his Olympian children.

His efforts were too late, however, as Metis was already pregnant with Athena. Metis would give birth in Zeus's belly, and she forged weapons and armor for her new daughter. Athena grew to adulthood and split the head of Zeus, springing forth from within armed and grown. Zeus, despite the manner of Athena's technical birth, came through the encounter unscathed.

Other traditions do exist where Athena was born as the mind of god. She still sprung from his forehead, but as a result of his intention of creating another world by use of the word logos.

Among her other attributions was that she was a patron of heroes. In Homer's Odyssey, she is impressed by the hero Odysseus as he tries to make his way toward his home of Ithaca. She could only assist him from afar, however, by implanting thoughts into his head on his travel back to his homeland.

Demeter was the goddess of the harvest. Of all the cults in ancient Greece, the cults of Demeter were possibly the most widespread and definitely the most secretive.

As the story of Demeter and Persephone is detailed in the book Ancient Greece of this series, it seems fitting to give a different account of the goddess's myth.

During her search for Persephone, Demeter took the form of an elderly mortal woman and called herself Doso. She was found by four daughters of the king of Eleusis, a man named Celeus. She claimed that she had been attacked by pirates, and entreated them to help her find work befitting an old woman.

Demeter asked the king for shelter, which he gave. He asked if she could nurse his children Triptolemus and Demophon. Demeter did the king one better. Due to his kindness and hospitality, she secretly began feeding Demophon ambrosia (the food of the gods), a substance which would grant immortality to those who partook of it. Then at night, she would hold the boy in the fire to cleanse him of his mortality.

When the queen of Eleusis, Celeus's wife Metanira stumbled across the scene, she took the situation at face value and screamed. Demeter abandoned her quest to make the boy immortal, and instead taught his brother the secrets of planting, harvesting and agriculture. This is, according to Greek mythology, how the people of the earth learned to grow crops.

Dionysus was the god of wine and merriment. He was born of a mortal woman named Semele. Hera, usually quick to discover her husband's infidelities, went to Semele as a nurse, or an old woman. Semele told the disguised goddess of the unborn child's father, that it was Zeus's child.

Hera encouraged Semele to doubt the Olympian heritage of her unborn child. Semele then went before the disguised Zeus and demanded that he reveal himself. When she persisted, he reluctantly agreed and showed himself in all of his glory. As an unconcealed god, the mortal woman could not survive the sight, and she died in flame.

Zeus, not wanting his child to also perish, removed the still developing child Dionysus from his dead mother's womb. To allow the boy to grow to full infancy, Zeus sewed Dionysus into his thigh. After a few months of incubation, Dionysus was born. Thus, he was a twice-born god, once of his mother Semele and once from the thigh of Zeus himself.

In another popular Dionysian tale, Silenus, Dionysus's foster father had passed out in the rose garden of a king. The king nursed him back to health for ten days. On the eleventh day, Silenus took the king to Dionysus who, being so grateful for Silenus's return and the hospitality of the king, offered the latter his choice of any reward that he so chose.

The king's name was Midas.

Hades was the god of the underworld. Despite modern depictions, Hades was not the most reviled of all the gods. In fact, during the Titanomachy, he fought bravely with the Olympians against their Titan foes. He was the oldest male childe of Cronus and Rhea and was therefore the last to be regurgitated by the former. This being the case, he can also technically be considered the youngest male (Hestia being the oldest {and youngest} of all the children).

While there was a later belief that Hades and Dionysus were one and the same, the people feared Hades. They would sacrifice black animals such as sheep to the underworld god and, as it was believed that the blood dripped through a crack in the earth, would avert their faces to avoid seeing him.

Hades took Persephone as his wife, but when Demeter refused to allow the crops of the earth to grow, she was returned for two-thirds of the year.

His chariot was led by four black horses, and he kept as a pet and guardian the three headed dog Cerberus.

Hephaestus, the god of fire, masonry and metal working, was the only one of the gods who was considered to be ugly. Born of Zeus and Hera, he often took his mother's side. In a particular argument of the espoused gods, Hephaestus stepped in between them. Zeus, furious at Hephaestus's intervention cast him out of Olympus, throwing him by the leg.

Hephaestus flew for the space of a full day, finally landing with an enormous impact on the island of Lemnos. He was nursed back to health, but would always walk with a limp. (although another version has Hera casting him out because he already had a withered foot.)

Despite being cast out, Hephaestus was able to regain his place on Olympus.

In order to prevent the other gods from fighting over who would be able to marry Aphrodite, Zeus arranged the marriage between the goddess of beauty and Hephaestus. Although he was considered to be the most balanced of the gods, the insatiable Aphrodite was constantly unfaithful.

Although she was married to Hephaestus, Aphrodite had a long-running romance with Ares. The two were spotted one day by Helios (the charioteer of the sun), who quickly made Hephaestus aware of the situation.

Rather than confront them outright, Hephaestus set a trap. He forged a net which was so fine it could not be seen by the naked eye. He set his trap and waited for its prey.

When Ares and Aphrodite were ensnared, Hephaestus brought forth the two naked gods to shame them before the others on Olympus. The other gods, however, only laughed at the sight. It wasn't until Poseidon persuaded Hephaestus to release the two by promising that Ares would pay the fine of the adulterer, that of returning the wife and reclaiming the price he had paid as dowry to Zeus.

Aphrodite not only laid with Hephaestus's brother Ares, but a prodigious string of gods and men. Hephaestus was hardly a pitiable cuckold though, as he fathered many children and had many consorts of his own.

Hephaestus worked the forges both on Olympus, and within the volcanos of the earth. To help him walk, he forged two robots out of metal (not joking) and endowed them with the gift of artificial intelligence. These two robots would serve as highly intelligent crutches to the god.

Hera was the queen of the Olympian gods, and goddess of marriage, birth and women. Her symbol was the peacock, and these birds were said to have drawn her chariot.

Much of the stories regarding Hera are in regard to her vengeance upon the women with whom her husband Zeus engaged in sexual intercourse, and her wrath against the children born of these affairs.

One of the most amusing stories about Hera and her infamous temper regards a man named Tiresias. When he was young, he came across the sight of two mating snakes, and struck them with a stick. His intervention caused a strange consequence though, as he was changed into a woman.

During his nine years as a female, he married and bore children. He also became a priestess of Hera. When he came across another instance of two snakes mating, he again struck them with a stick and returned to his original male form.

In what can only be called an Olympian parlor bet, Zeus and Hera confronted Tiresias, asking him for whom sex was more pleasurable, men or women. The two gods believed that it was the sex opposite of theirs who enjoyed the greater ecstasy. Tiresias answered that sexual intercourse was more pleasurable for women. Enraged at the answer, Tiresias was struck blind by Hera.

Zeus could not restore Tiresias's sight; however, he did give him the gift of prophetic sight.

Hermes was the messenger of the gods. He was the son of Zeus and Maia. Among his other attributions, he was also the god of thieves, trade, athletes. He also guided souls to the underworld.

Hermes was a notorious trickster. While still an infant, he leapt from his cradle and hid Apollo's cattle. Apollo realized what was happening and confronted the child. Hermes insisted that he had nothing to do with it, so Apollo brought him before Zeus in a rage. Zeus, however, thought the matter was hilarious.

Like many of the other Olympians, Hermes was quite the philanderer. He never married, but fathered many children with over forty different women and goddesses.

He was also a patron to inventors, and is said to have invented music, numbers, the alphabet, astronomy, measurement, and many other indispensable creations.

Hestia was the goddess of architecture, the hearth and home, domesticity and the family. She was a daughter of Cronus and Rhea. She was a passive goddess, and is not always considered to be one of the twelve. In other myths, Dionysus replaces her on Olympus.

She remained a virgin, despite the advances of Apollo and Poseidon. She was directed by Zeus to tend the

Olympian fires. With any sacrifice, as Hestia was the oldest child of Cronus and Rhea (and the last to be purged, therefore also the youngest), Hestia was the first goddess to receive an offering.

Persephone was the daughter of Demeter and Zeus, and consort of Hades. Thus she was the goddess of the underworld. She is identified with the growth and productivity of the seasons, due to the above mentioned abduction and residence with Hades during what are the winter months.

Every spring as she returned from the underworld, the plant life would spring back up. As she was symbolically reborn, so were crops and other plants which had lain dormant in during her time in the underworld.

Poseidon was the god of the seas, earthquakes, storms, etc. His weapon (and symbol) was the trident. Another bisexual god, Poseidon had many consorts and children. He was often referred to as the earth shaker, and was one of the Olympian gods who fought against the Titans.

He was in competition against Athena to be the patron god of Athens. Although he lost the contest, he would remain a chief deity among the Athenians.

In Homer's Odyssey, he was angry with Odysseus (or Ulysses in Latin) for blinding one of his children, a

Cyclops. The god of the sea was infuriated, and set about making Odysseus's journey as difficult as possible. He, in fact, tried to kill Odysseus on more than one occasion, but was always thwarted.

Although much has already been covered in regard to Zeus (and much more will be covered) it seems fitting to give some information about the god outside of his poisoning his father Cronus, and his various infidelities.

Although the primary focus thus far has been on Zeus's various indiscretions (an accounting of his romantic endeavors alone would fill a few volumes), Zeus also had a protective side, especially toward Hera.

Ixion, king of the Lapiths in Thessaly, would come across Zeus in a way which was new to mortals of the time. According to myth, Ixion had married the daughter of Eioneus, but didn't pay the dowry. Eioneus, in order to have some assurance that Ixion would come to pay him, held his son-in-law's horses as collateral to ensure that payment would be made.

Ixion, however, was not about to give his new father-in-law his just dues. He lured Eioneus to his home, saying that he was ready to pay up, but killed Eioneus by casting into a flaming pit.

Killing a member of one's own family, in the myth, was unheard of, and those who could purify him refused to do so. Zeus, taking pity on the mortal invited Ixion to his table at Olympus, but Ixion's treachery was not over.

Ixion became enamored with, and began to pursue Hera. When Hera told Zeus about this, the king of the gods could hardly believe that one, especially someone in Ixion's position, would be so impudent as to make a move on his wife.

Zeus, as a test, created a cloud in the form of Hera (who would come to be called Nephele) and placed it in Ixion's bed (other stories have the cloud-Hera being placed in Hera's bed). Ixion had imbibed a few drinks at this point, and when he came across Nephele, he set himself upon it.

Zeus came in and, unable to deny Ixion's motives any longer, cast Ixion from Olympus, striking him with a thunderbolt. Ixion was bound to a flaming wheel, which was set to spin for eternity.

According to the myth, Nephele (cloud-Hera) had become pregnant through the dalliance with Ixion and gave birth to Centauros. Centauros would go on to mate with the horses of Mount Pelion, thus creating the race of Centaurs.

These are but a few stories related to the gods. The myths surrounding most of them are quite vast, and their essences are still about us today in popular and underground culture.

# CHAPTER 4

*Heracles and the Twelve Labors*

Zeus (as is well established by now) was quite the playboy. How he ever got anything done between his affairs is astounding. However, one of his many children would come to be known as the divine hero. Quite possibly the most famous of Zeus's mortal children would be the one known as Heracles.

Heracles (the original figure from whom Hercules was adapted) was the son of Zeus and Alcmene. Zeus disguised himself as Alcmene's husband, Amphitryon, returning from the war of the time. He lied with her and swiftly departed. Later on that same evening, the real Amphitryon returned home. His wife, already impregnated by Zeus with Heracles, became pregnant that same night with the child of Amphitryon.

The hatred of Hera toward Heracles is legendary. This began its manifestation during Alcmene's pregnancy. Hera convinced Zeus to declare that the next high king would be of the house (a descendant of) Perseus (the founder of Mycenae, and the hero who beheaded the gorgon Medusa). Unbeknownst to Zeus, another child of that house was nearing its birth.

To ensure that the product of Zeus's infidelity would not become high king as intended, Hera went to Ilithyia, the goddess of childbirth, and tied Ilithyia's clothing in knots, her legs crossed. As no mortal could be born with Ilithyia in such a position without the intervention of a god, Heracles and his unborn twin half-brother were stuck in the womb of Alcmene.

Hera, in order to ensure the succession of another high king, caused the child Eurystheus to be born prematurely. He was now the one destined to become the high king while Heracles and his brother remained unborn.

Hera never intended for Heracles to be born at all. It was when one of Alcmene's servants came to Ilithyia and lied to the goddess, saying that the twins had indeed been born. Ilithyia, overcome by surprise, reacted with such a startled gesticulation at the news that her bonds were broken, thus allowing the twins to be born.

Alcmene offered up the child Heracles in an attempt to escape the goddess's wrath, however, when he was brought before her by Athena, Hera didn't know the child's identity. She nursed him, but the child's incredible strength caused Hera pain while nursing.

She removed the suckling child from her breast (the milk coming out to form the Milky Way).

Though Hera cast the child aside, he had consumed some of the milk, and with that, he acquired his powers. He was brought back to the house of Alcmene, and would be raised by them. Still fearing Hera's wrath, the child (who had originally been named Alcides by his mortal parents) was renamed Heracles.

This was not to be the end of Hera's attempts on the boy, however. When he was less than one year old, Hera sent two snakes to kill the young Heracles. Although his brother cowered, Heracles took the beasts to be playthings. He strangled them and played with them in his crib.

Heracles would grow to adulthood and marry a woman named Megara. The two had children, and life was good until Hera decided to intervene yet again. Sources differ upon exactly when, but what is consistent is that Hera caused Heracles to go insane. He believed that he was being attacked by evil spirits. He fought back against these dark beings, the battle ending in their easy slaughter. The problem was, these were no demons. In his madness, he had killed his children (in some myths he also killed Megara, however others have her departing and marrying his charioteer and nephew Iolaus).

Just as he was about to kill his mortal pater Amphitryon, Athena, known for her protectiveness of heroes, cast a stone into Heracles's chest, causing him to lose consciousness.

Now guilty of a sin which would require absolution, Heracles went before the oracle of Delphi, not knowing that the oracle was under the influence of his evil step-mother (history has a lot of those) Hera. The oracle advised Heracles to go before the high king and serve him in whatever way he should require. If he did so, Heracles was promised immortality, and a seat at Olympus.

The high king Eurystheus, an ally of Hera, was all too eager to have such a mighty servant. Although Eurystheus originally said that the debt of Heracles would be considered cleansed after performing ten heroic tasks, his requirements of the budding hero would come to be known as the twelve labors of Heracles.

The first labor was to kill the Nemean Lion, a ferocious beast with nearly impenetrable skin. Not only this, he was given only thirty days to complete the task. Let's just say Heracles and Eurystheus had issues. Heracles gathered arrows in order to slay the lion but the arrows bounced harmlessly from the lion's tough hide. Stories differ on whether he was finally able to strangle the lion to death, or whether he shot an arrow through the lion's mouth. Regardless, Heracles had indeed passed his first test.

Heracles tried to skin the lion, but could not break through its thick skin. It was only when Athena guided him to use the lion's own claws, that he was able to achieve the task. Heracles skinned the lion, and fashioned a cloak of armor from its impenetrable hide.

The king, upon seeing Heracles returning and carrying the dead beast on the thirtieth day, was petrified. He forbade Heracles to enter the city again, and communicated the remainder of the tasks through use of a messenger.

The second labor of Heracles was to slay the Lernaean Hydra, a nine headed serpent. The hydra was spawned by Hera (surprise, surprise) in order to kill Heracles. Slaying the beast would prove to be an even more difficult trial than the Nemean lion.

The Bibliotheca (fallaciously attributed to Apollodorus) gives a detailed account of the bout. The hydra *began* with nine heads, poisonous breath and even its tracks could kill a man. Heracles covered his mouth and nose to protect himself from the miasma of poisonous gas.

Heracles quickly went to work, decapitating the heads of the hydra one-by-one. Much to his dismay, however, with every beheading, the hydra would sprout two to replace the stump. He called for his charioteer (some say nephew) Iolaus for help. A new approach was developed including both of the men. Heracles would sever each head, and Iolaus would quickly cauterize the stump before two new heads could be sprouted.

This method worked quite effectively, although Hera wasn't done yet. She sent forth a crab to distract Heracles so that the hydra would be able to defeat the hero. Heracles, undaunted, stomped the crab beneath his foot.

The final head of the hydra became immortal, however Heracles was able to sever it with the use of a golden sword which Athena had given to him. The beast was slain. Heracles, always an opportunist, dipped the tips of his arrows in the blood of the poisonous blood of the hydra.

Unfortunately for Heracles, upon completing his tenth task, Eurystheus declared the slaying of the hydra improperly completed as the hero had the help of his nephew and charioteer.

The third task of Heracles was to be different. Heracles had proven himself against the fiercest of Hera's creations, and so Eurystheus set the next task to be the capturing of the Ceryneian Hind, an animal sacred to Artemis, able to outrun an arrow.

Heracles awoke one morning to glimpse the light reflected from one of its antlers. He gave chase to the animal, but it was indefatigable. He would chase it for the space of one year.

He eventually caught it, but on his return was confronted by Artemis and her brother Apollo. Heracles quickly explained and apologized for the situation. Artemis agreed to forgive him, so long as he let it go upon proving the hind's capture. Heracles agreed and, upon reaching the gates of the city, insisted that Eurystheus come and behold the animal for himself.

When Eurystheus came outside the city gates, Heracles, true to his promise let the hind go. He taunted Eurystheus, saying that the king had been too sluggish, and that it was his fault that the hind had escaped. It's not like the two were friends, but Eurystheus became more determined than ever to foil the hero's quest to become immortal.

The fourth labor of Heracles was to capture the Erymanthian Boar. He consulted a centaur for guidance, and was told to lead the boar into thick snow. By these means, he was able to capture the animal. He returned to the centaur. The centaur was overcome with fear at the sight of it. He begged Heracles to dispose of the boar, and Heracles obliged.

As the fifth labor, Eurystheus decided to not only present Heracles with a near impossible task, but to humiliate him in the process. The fifth labor was to clean the stables of Augeas in one day. Augeas, no doubt excited to learn that his stables would finally be cleaned, offered Heracles one-tenth of his herd, should the hero be able to finish the job in the space of a day.

While certainly being demeaning work, Eurystheus felt that the labor would be futile, as the stable housed over a thousand immortal cattle which produced an epic amount of droppings. To add further difficulty, the stables had not been cleaned in over thirty years.

Heracles, always persistent, rerouted two rivers, the Peneus and the Alpheus to run through the stables, thus washing them clean. Augeas, thinking the task impossible in such a short time-frame, rescinded his offer to the hero, claiming that he had already been instructed to carry out the cleaning anyway. In many myths, upon completion of his labors, Heracles would return to kill the reneging stable-owner.

After his tenth labor was complete, Eurystheus would declare this task to be forfeit as the slaying of the hydra, due to the fact that it was not Heracles, but the rivers which cleaned the stables.

The sixth labor of Heracles was to kill or drive away the Stymphalian birds. These, true to form, were no ordinary birds, but creatures with bronze beaks, and metallic feathers which the birds could use as projectiles to fend off any possible predators. And, as if Heracles hadn't waded through enough feces, the droppings of the birds were poisonous.

Heracles went to the swamp where the birds dwelled, however, he was unable to make his way closer to them as he would sink in the soft ground. Athena came to the rescue once again, presenting Heracles with a rattle, made by Hephaestus. Upon shaking it, the birds were frightened and took wing. He killed many of them with his bow, while the rest would fly away.

The seventh labor was to capture, but not kill, the Cretan bull. This bull had been causing all sorts of havoc in Crete. The king of the time (mythical King Minos) was quick to offer his aid, but Heracles refused. He was able to come up behind the bull and beat it to within an inch of its life.

He had the bruised and beaten bull sent back to Eurystheus who intended to sacrifice it to Hera. The goddess, however, refused the sacrifice, and Eurystheus let the beast go.

The eighth labor was to capture Diomedes's horses. The task may have seemed simple at first, but Heracles soon came to the knowledge that the mares were wild, likely caused by a steady diet of human flesh.

Diomedes was hardly keen to have his horses taken. In a common version of the myth, Heracles refused to sleep during the night, fearing that Diomedes would try to kill him in his sleep. He snuck in and severed the chains which held the horses.

He then spooked them to the top of a peninsula, took his axe and cut the land around the peninsula and thus trapped the horses on his self-made island. Heracles killed Diomedes and fed him to his horses which calmed the man-eaters down enough for the hero to bind their mouths and return them to Eurystheus.

The ninth labor was a task for the petulant king's petulant daughter. She coveted the girdle of Hyppolyta, the queen of the Amazons, and so her father Eurystheus commanded the retrieval of the belt to be the ninth labor.

Heracles set sail with some of his companions and, upon landing on the shores of the Amazon's territory, told the Amazonian queen of his task. The queen was impressed, and offered to give the girdle to Heracles without protest, even though it had been a gift to her by the god of war Ares.

Hera, however, just couldn't stay out of things, and disguised herself, slandering Heracles to the Amazons. She told them that his real purpose was to kidnap their queen and the Amazons quickly attacked him and his ship.

Heracles fought off the Amazons, killing their queen and taking the girdle from around her. He set sail, and delivered the belt to Eurystheus.

The tenth labor (which was supposed to be his last) was for Heracles to return with the cattle of the monster Geryon. This task was in a far off land, and so Heracles had to do some traveling.

He reached the desert of Libya and, while trudging through it, became angry at the excessive heat. To vent his displeasure, he shot an arrow at Helios, the Titan who carried the sun through the sky. While the arrow missed its target, Helios was so impressed by the feat that he offered his golden cup to assist Heracles in his travels through the desert. This cup was the means of by which Helios made his conveyance from the west (at the end of the day) to the east (to begin the next day). By using this cup, Heracles was able to reach the land of Erytheia where Geyron and his cattle lived.

Upon disembarking, Heracles encountered a two-headed dog named Orthrus. He made short work of the animal, killing it with his club. The herdsman in charge of the cattle tried to join Orthrus in fending off the hero, but was himself slain.

Alerted by the sounds of fighting, Geryon sprang into action. The monster, depending on the source, either had three heads and one body, or one head and three bodies, either two or six legs; various combinations of Geryon's anatomy are recorded.

The monster donned his armor and set off to attack Heracles. The hero, however, shot Geryon with one of his hydra-poisoned arrows with a force that sent the arrow through the monster's forehead, killing him.

Now at his leisure, Heracles collected the cattle and traveled back to Eurystheus. In one version of the story, the cattle are stolen by a giant named Cacus while Heracles is sleeping. The giant dragged the cattle backward so as to confuse the hero, should he go looking for them.

Heracles would find the trail, finding a cave with an enormous stone set in front of it (by Cacus). Heracles, quite the strong figure himself simply tore the top from the mountain and did battle with the giant. He slayed his foe, but Hera turned herself into a gadfly and proceeded to bite the cattle, causing them to scatter. Over the space of a year, Heracles would find all of the cattle, and so he made his way back to Eurystheus, thinking it to be for the last time.

Eurystheus, however, rejected two of the labors (the killing of the hydra and the cleaning of the stables), and insisted that Heracles was not yet finished. He therefore set two more tasks ahead of the hero.

The eleventh labor of Heracles was to gather the golden apples from the garden of Hesperides. The Hesperides were nymphs who tended the garden where the golden apples grew. According to one myth, these golden apples would grant the one who ate of them immortality for the space of one day. An individual could, in theory, eat an apple a day and become immortal. (There's a rhyme in that somewhere).

Upon reaching the garden, Heracles came across Anteus, a being who was immortal unless he was separated from his mother Gaia. Heracles, upon discovering this, lifted his foe from the ground and crushed him in his strong arms.

Heracles reached the garden, but was unable to retrieve the apples on his own. He went to Atlas, the Titan holding up the sky, and made a deal with him. Heracles would hold up the sky and Atlas would receive a rest from his duties for the time it took the Titan to retrieve the apples (I think we see where this is going). Atlas quickly agreed and Heracles took to holding Uranus from Gaia.

Upon Atlas's return, however, the Titan refused to return to his post. Heracles, not willing to give up his quest and acquiesce to being the new form of separation between the sky and the earth, tricked Atlas into resuming his duty by asking the Titan if he would hold the sky long enough for Heracles to adjust his cloak. Atlas agreed (and I think we see where this one's going too) and Heracles quickly made off with the apples.

The hero returned, giving Eurystheus the golden apples, ready for his twelfth and final labor.

The twelfth labor of Heracles was to capture, but not kill Cerberus, the three-headed dog which guarded the underworld. Heracles was also not allowed to use any weapons in the tri-headed dog's capture.

The hero set out. He went to Eleusis in order to gain the knowledge of how to enter and exit the underworld while retaining his life. With the help of Hermes and Athena, he was able to enter the gates of the underworld at Tanaerum. He traversed the river Styx and, upon arriving in the underworld, opened up a dialog with Hades.

Hades agreed to allow Heracles to take Cerberus so long as he could capture the dog(s) without hurting him, and return the guardian dog(s) safely after the labor was complete. Heracles agreed.

Either before or after his conversation with Hades, Heracles came upon two men who were bound to chairs in the underworld. The men were Pirithious and Thesius, two men who had endeavored to kidnap Persephone so that Pirithious could take her as his wife.

Heracles was able to wrest Thesius from his chair, leaving a portion of the latter's thigh. Heracles was unsuccessful freeing Pirithious, however. It was said that the attempt shook the earth.

Heracles would finally come upon Cerberus. He was able to capture the Cerberus and didn't harm the dog in the process. He took Cerberus before Eurystheus, but when the king beheld the guardian of the underworld, he is said to have died of fright. (According to some myths, he simply cowered and told Heracles to return the dog to the underworld). Regardless what happened to Eurystheus, Heracles was now free of his debt for killing his children (and possibly wife).

The journey of Heracles was far from over, but he was finally free.

# CHAPTER 5

*Other Important Beings in Structure of Greek Mythology*

The mythos of the Greeks was not limited to the major gods and the demigods (such as Heracles). A number of other characters would find an important role in the belief system of the ancient Greeks.

Prometheus was the most important character in regard to humankind, for he was their creator. The son of the Clymene and the Titan Iapetus, Prometheus did not participate in the direct conflict between the Titans and the Olympian gods (in other versions, he fought on the side of the Olympians). He was, therefore, spared their fate.

Prometheus fashioned the first human beings out of clay or mud and showed his creations to the goddess Athena. The goddess was so impressed that she breathed life into them. Thrilled by his creations being given life, Prometheus would teach the humans everything that he knew of math, science, and civilization. This would cause the first rift between Zeus and Prometheus.

Zeus, upset by Prometheus's indiscretion of teaching the humans the knowledge of the gods, made humankind mortal and cast them away from Mount Olympus.

At a dinner between gods and mortals, Prometheus presented Zeus with an option of two meals. One meal was that of an ox (unbeknownst to Zeus, Prometheus had set a meal of beef in the stomach of the ox), the other was that of gleaming fat (beneath which, Zeus would find only bare bones). Zeus, tantalized by the fatty plate, chose it as his meal. When he discovered that the plate was made up of bones which had been stripped of their meat, Zeus became furious with Prometheus.

Prometheus also gave humans fire. Accounts differ as to whether the humans already had the use of fire, but were stripped of it after Prometheus's fat and bones trick on the king of gods, or whether they didn't have fire in the first place. What is common though, is that Zeus at one point forbade the humans to be allowed the use of fire.

Seeing his creations suffering, Prometheus stole away the fire of the gods which Zeus had hidden and presented it to the humans, giving them (or returning to them) the use of flame.

For this, Zeus would levy one of his most extreme punishments. He had Prometheus chained to a rock where every day an eagle (a symbol of Zeus) would devour his liver. At night, the liver of Prometheus would regrow, allowing this cycle to continue on eternally.

Depending on the version of the myth, Prometheus was never freed from his bondage or, in some versions, was unchained by Heracles.

*Perseus and Medusa*

Medusa is, no doubt, one of the most familiar figures from Greek mythology. What is often not known about her is that she was once a stunningly beautiful, virginal priestess of Athena, the goddess of war and wisdom.

As Athena was a virgin, so too were all of her priestesses. Medusa had many suitors, but always held firm to her oaths of chastity. It was not only mortal men, however, that found Medusa irresistible.

The god Poseidon came to Medusa while she was inside Athena's temple on the hill of the acropolis. He viciously attacked and raped her. The act was not only a heinous violation of the young priestess, but a sacrilege to Athena.

Athena, however, did not take the side of her priestess. For the crime of *being* raped, Athena placed a terrible curse upon Medusa. Her skin was cracked and aged, her beauty turned to hideousness, her long hair was transformed into snakes and all who looked upon her would be turned to stone. Medusa was transformed into a gorgon.

Medusa was cast into exile, but quickly became hunted. According to the myth, even after Medusa was slain, her head would still cause any who looked upon her to turn to stone. Warriors came from all around to capture this tactical prize, only to be turned to stone in Medusa's growing rock garden.

Medusa would meet her match, however, at the hands of a warrior named Perseus. Danaë, the mother of Perseus, had been locked into a stone tower by her father Acrisius, the king of Argos. With no male heir, Acrisius consulted an oracle to discover whether his daughter would bear a grandson. The oracle instructed Acrisius that if Danaë were to become pregnant, her son would one day kill him and take his throne.

The theme of the older generation fearing their overthrow by a younger generation has persisted throughout the world, not only in myth and culture, but in real life as well.

Acrisius, fearing his as yet unconceived grandson, locked Danaë into the stone tower, expecting her to die from starvation as she was given very little food. The one thing that Acrisius hadn't prepared for, however, was the attention of the gods.

Zeus, always the philanderer, came through the window as a shower of gold. He impregnated Danaë with a son. When the news of his daughter's death never came, Acrisius went to investigate, finding his daughter holding her newly born child Perseus.

Afraid of offending Zeus, he didn't dare kill the two outright; however, he placed Danaë into a boat and set her adrift in the sea. They would eventually land on the island of Serifos. As Perseus grew, the king of Serifos became enamored with his mother. Hating Perseus, the king demanded that all occupants of Serifos provide him with a lavish gift; those who did not would be banished.

As Perseus was poor, the king expected him to be unable to present a fitting gift. In order to prevent the king from taking his mother as his wife and banishing him, Perseus promised the king that he would bring as his offering the head of Medusa.

The problem for Perseus was that he not only lacked any weapons, armor or knowledge of what Medusa looked like (as any who had actually seen her form would have been turned to stone), he also had no idea where he was going.

He prayed to the gods and, having heard his prayer, Zeus sent forth Hermes who gave the young man a pair of winged sandals. Hermes then told Perseus of a group of nymphs who would help him further. In order to find the nymphs, Perseus had to confront the Graeae, sisters of the gorgons.

The Graeae were three beings who shared use of one eyeball. In order to gain their cooperation, Perseus snatched the eyeball from the sisters and demanded that they tell him how to reach the grove of the nymphs. This was the same garden which Heracles encountered while searching for the golden apples.

Upon reaching the grove, the nymphs gave him a satchel within which Perseus could store the severed head of Medusa without fear of being turned to stone. Before he reached Medusa though, he would require much more.

He gained the necessary items by the kindness of the gods. Hades provided Perseus with a helm of darkness; Zeus gave Perseus an adamantine sword; and Athena gave Perseus the polished shield which would become iconic of the hero.

Now very well prepared for the confrontation, Perseus traveled to the island where Medusa had been exiled. By walking backward, he was able to view Medusa by looking at her reflection through the polished shield that Athena gave to him. By this means, he was able to sneak up on her and cut off her head.

When Perseus returned to the island of Serifos, he found his mother about to be married to the king against her will. The king had been making violent advances toward Danaë, and so Perseus, always protective of his mother used Medusa's head on the foul king. Acrisius had also come to attend the wedding and, justly enough, he too caught a glimpse of the gorgon's head.

Perseus would eventually offer Medusa's head to Athena as a tribute.

## The Minotaur

Son of a human mother and a bull father, the Minotaur was one of the most feared of all the monsters in ancient Greece. Residing in a labyrinth on the island of Crete, the Minotaur lied in wait for a prisoner to enter its dwelling. Once found, the victim would be torn limb from limb and devoured by the ravenous beast.

The Minotaur was brought into being by an offense toward the god Poseidon by the king of Crete, Minos. The king had prayed to Poseidon to send a white bull, showing him favor and as the rightful heir to the throne of Crete. Upon its arrival, Minos had promised to sacrifice the bull to Poseidon; however, having become an admirer of the beauty of the bull, Minos reneged. (In another version of this story, Minos would slaughter the most prized new calf every year to Poseidon, but when the white bull was born, he couldn't bring himself to sacrifice it. Instead he slaughtered another bull, thinking that the god would call it even).

What is consistent in the myths is Poseidon's reaction to the sleight. He caused Minos's wife, Queen Pasiphaë to fall in love with the bull. The queen longed to copulate with the beast. She commissioned a great inventor named Daedalus to build her a wooden cow, hollow on the inside.

The queen took the decoy into the pasture where the bull lived, climbed inside and the rest is best left to the imagination. She became pregnant and, upon her delivery, the Minotaur (or bull of Minos) was born.

In an effort to turn lemons into lemonade, Minos decided to use the Minotaur to his own advantage. He commissioned Daedalus to envision and build a prison wherein the Minotaur would be placed, and any prisoners would be forced to face it.

Androgeus the son of Minos was in Athens, competing in Panathenaic Games, an early predecessor to the Olympics. He won every event, angering the other competitors. These men killed him. When Minos heard of this, he declared war on Athens.

In lieu of a full on attack, Minos demanded that seven male virgins and seven female virgins be offered to him as tribute to be sacrificed to the Minotaur once every nine years. This repeated until the third cycle when Theseus, son of not only the king and queen of Athens, but of Poseidon as well.

Having this dual paternity allowed Theseus to be an heir to the Athenian throne and also possess some of the powers of the gods. When he grew, the third set of virgins was rounded up, and he joined with them, vowing to bring down the terrible beast which had killed those sent before him. Having grown enough to retrieve his father's sword from beneath a boulder (where Aegeus, the king of Athens and father of Theseus had placed it), Aegeus had only one request of his son. Should he survive and return home, he should raise the white sail instead of the black sail in order to show his father that he lived.

When Theseus arrived at Knossos, the capitol of Crete, he quickly caught the eye of Ariadne, the daughter of king Minos. She fell in love with him and went to Daedalus in order to find some way to help the young man return from his imprisonment in the labyrinth. Daedalus gave her a clue (or ball of string) so that she could offer Theseus a way back to the entrance of the maze. She had one condition though. If Theseus survived, he would have to agree to marry her. Theseus agreed.

The fourteen virgins were led the next morning to the entrance of the labyrinth and locked inside. With his ball of twine, Theseus would lead the way. He bore the sword of Aegeus, and made his way in the dark through the labyrinth, searching for the Minotaur.

By the time his clue was one-quarter the size it had been upon his entry, Theseus comes across the sleeping Minotaur. Theseus ambushes the bull-headed creature, catching him off guard. The two would do battle: the Minotaur wielding an axe, Theseus with a sword.

The two do battle, but Theseus quickly has the upper hand. He corners the Minotaur and is able to slay him, but he's not out of the woods yet. Day is approaching and, should Theseus and the other virgins be caught by king Minos, they will surely be slain. He quickly makes his way back through the labyrinth, following the string that Ariadne had given him. Theseus and the others would escape in the dark of the night. Before dawn arrived, Ariadne met Theseus on the Athenian's boat and the group set sail toward Athens.

Aegeus, Theseus's father, had gone to a cliff overlooking the sea every day in order to ascertain his son's fate. When the ship came into view, Theseus had neglected to raise the white sail. Aegeus, thinking his son to be dead was so distraught that he cast himself over the cliff and to his death. These waters would come to be called the Aegean Sea.

# CHAPTER 6

*Greek Mythology and Homer's Iliad and Odyssey*

Before ending, the myths and legends described by Homer in Iliad and Odyssey bear some investigation.

The stories of Homer's Iliad and Odyssey were originally communicated through word of mouth by travelling bards. They were collected by Homer (and possibly altered to fit into Homer's own sense of the story). While a brief synopsis of each will be given here, I also encourage you to read these two epics. They have been an inspiration in culture and literature since their original telling, over 2,500 years ago.

## Iliad

Homer's Iliad begins near the end of the Trojan War. The Achaeans (or Greeks) are battling the Trojans. A priest of Apollo offers Agamemnon, the king of the Achaeans, vast wealth in exchange for Agamemnon to return his daughter Chryseis. Agamemnon refuses.

The priest then prays to Apollo for help and guidance and the god, a patron of Troy, sends forth a plague into the Greek camp which claims many lives. This plague continues for the space of nine days, until Achilles, hero of the Greeks and leader of the legendary Myrmidons, demands that Agamemnon return the girl to her father and end the plague.

While Agamemnon agrees to return Chryseis, he takes Briseis, a captive of Achilles, as recompense. Achilles is enraged and from that point refuses to fight. He also orders his Myrmidons to stand down. They threaten to leave the battle and the beach near Troy altogether. Meanwhile, Odysseus returns Chryseis to her father, thus ending the plague on the Greeks.

Mutinous, Achilles bids his mother Thetis, a goddess of the sea, to beseech Zeus and ask him to fight on the side of the Trojans. He does this in order to either convince Agamemnon to appreciate how much he needs Achilles and his Myrmidons, or bring a swifter end to the war. Zeus agrees, and the tide is turned.

Agamemnon has a dream that night, sent by Zeus, instructing him to attack the city walls. Upon his awakening, Agamemnon decided to test the morale of his soldiers by telling them all to head home. With the recent plague and the refusal of Achilles and his Myrmidons to fight, the soldiers were very nearly routed. It was only by the intervention of Athena, through the mouth and actions of Odysseus that the Greeks remained. He challenged and killed a discontented soldier for airing his grievances about the continued combat.

Word of the Greeks' pending attack reaches Priam (king of Troy) who then sets his own men out to the battlefield. As the armies approached each other, Paris, the prince of Troy and man who had stolen Helen from the Greek Minelaus, the act which purportedly started the war, (see previous chapter's section regarding Paris and the three goddesses), offered to fight a duel with the vastly superior warrior Minelaus to decide the victor of the war. Paris was no match for Minelaus, but was spared by Aphrodite before he could be killed.

At the intervention of Zeus, an arrow takes flight and wounds Minelaus, thus breaking the temporary truce and rejoining the battle. One of the great warriors on the side of the Greeks is Diomedes. He kills many soldiers, including Pandaros, the man who released the arrow wounding Minelaus. Aphrodite intervenes, but is wounded by Diomedes. Apollo then comes forth and warns Diomedes against battling against the gods, but the latter is not dissuaded.

The gods of Olympus were split in regard to their support of the armies, and Diomedes wounds yet another deity, Ares, who shrieks out in a very un-war-god-like cry (see above section on Ares).

After rallying his forces, Hector (brother of Paris and prince of Troy) reenters the city to bid the people toward prayer and sacrifice. He returns to the battle and confronts Ajax, a mighty Greek warrior. The two fight to a stalemate as the sun goes down.

The next day, the two armies agree to a day's peace so that they can burn their dead. The Greeks also erect a wall for protection. Paris refuses to return Helen over the protestation of many of the Trojans. He offers instead to return a treasure he had stolen and much of his own riches, but this offer is in vain.

Upon the next morning, the gods are forbidden by Zeus to interfere in the battle. The Trojans are victorious on the day and drive the Greeks back to their encampment. The sun goes down and prevents the Trojans from assailing the walls, so instead, they camp on the field.

Meanwhile, Agamemnon is ready to do whatever necessary to convince Achilles to return to the battle. He sends two heralds along with the Greek warriors Odysseus, Phoenix and Ajax who also bear gifts to Achilles. The Myrmidon warrior refuses to return to battle unless the Trojans breach the Greek walls and attack their camps and ships with fire.

During the night, Diomedes and Odysseus kill a Trojan warrior and generally cause mayhem among the camps of the Trojan allies. When morning comes, Hector leads the charge against the Greeks. He is begged not to proceed by Polydamas, an oracle, but the prince continues onward.

Zeus, who had continued to prohibit the gods from interference, is lured to sleep by Hera so that Poseidon can intervene on the side of the Greeks. Upon waking, Zeus sends forth Apollo on the side of the Trojans to sway the tide of the battle back in the favor of the Trojans. Unfortunately for the Trojans, they reach the ships and cause Achilles to send his friend Patroclus into battle wearing his armor to rally the Greek soldiers.

The tide of the battle is again turned, and Patroclus kills one of the Trojan heroes, sending the Trojans into retreat. He pursues the Trojans back to the city walls and is confronted by Apollo himself. Patroclus is killed by Hector, thinking the warrior to be Achilles.

Hector takes the armor of Achilles as his own and chaos breaks out.

The news of his slain friend is enough to enrage Achilles. He swears vengeance on the prince of Troy and he stands at the gate of the Grecian walls and, inspired by Athena, thunders in rage at the Trojan army. The Trojans are terrified by the presence of Achilles and in the cacophony, the Greeks are able to retrieve the body of Patroclus, and they bring his remains back to their camp.

New armor is fashioned by Hephaestus, and Achilles dons the gifts, ready to avenge his friend by killing the Trojan prince Hector. The next morning comes, and Agamemnon again offers Achilles gifts, including the return of Briseis, but Achilles has only one thing on his mind: his revenge on Hector.

Though Achilles is aware that he is destined to die young, and is even warned by his horse of his own coming death, the warrior drives his chariot into battle. He slaughters the Trojans before him and, splitting off about half of the Trojan forces, proceeds to slaughter this entire group. He is confronted by the river god Skamandros, who is upset that Achilles had littered his waters with so many dead Trojans. The god is driven back, however and Achilles returns to battle.

The gods, having been released by Zeus from their bonds of non-interference, rejoin the battle. Achilles is tricked by the god Apollo and led away from the mass of the Trojan forces as they retreat into the city. Only Hector remains outside the city walls.

Despite his initial urge to stand and fight, as Achilles draws closer, Hector begins to run around the walls of Troy, trying to evade the hero. He runs until Athena intervenes, fooling the prince into facing Achilles. The battle doesn't last long.

Achilles ties Hector's body to the back of his chariot and drags the prince's corpse back to the Greek camp. Despite being visited in a dream by his friend Patroclus who urges Achilles to bury Hector and allow the usual honors to fall to the slain prince, Achilles continues to desecrate the body by riding it around the funeral pyre of Patroclus.

Having had enough of this, Zeus sends Hermes to bring Priam to the tent of Achilles. Though initially confused by the Trojan king's presence, Priam's pleas compel Achilles to release Hector's body to the king. It is with the funeral of Hector that Homer's Iliad comes to an end.

## Odyssey

The chronology of Iliad and Odyssey skips a number of years and a few important events which bear a mention albeit brief here. The city of Troy would fall to the Greek soldiers after Odysseus hatched a cunning plan during the funeral games for Hector, son of Priam.

The idea was to build a great wooden horse and present it as if it were a gift to the Trojans, honoring the god Poseidon. The Trojans brought the horse through their gate and into the city. Now unhindered, the Greeks only needed to wait until nightfall to spring from inside the horse and overtake the city.

The plan worked nearly to perfection; however, Paris, the one who caused the war and who cowered before Minelaus, shot Achilles through the heel with a poisoned arrow, killing him. Alternatively, one version of the story has Paris stabbing Achilles in the back while the latter was being married to Polyxena, one of Priam's daughters. Either way, Paris's slaying of Achilles never bears him any honor, and Achilles goes to his grave having never been defeated in battle.

Homer's Odyssey begins ten years since the end of the Trojan War and Odysseus has yet to return to his native Ithaca where he is king. The Odyssey is told, quite often, through the use of flashbacks. When the text begins, he is actually near the end of his journey, but the text reveals the ins and outs of his travels and tribulations.

Back at home, his wife Penelope is constantly beset by one-hundred and eight different suitors. These men believe Odysseus to be dead, and are quick to pounce on the opportunity for free food, drink, and the chance to possibly become king of Ithaca.

Penelope, while she despises the suitors, is bound by convention to feed these vultures. She refuses to take one as her husband, but can't turn them away either.

Much of the first books which make up Homer's Odyssey involve Telemachus, the son of Odysseus and Penelope. Athena, Odysseus's greatest ally disguises herself and tells Telemachus to search for information about his father's fate. Athena also approaches Zeus around this time, conveniently when Poseidon is not around. She would further help the young man by securing a ship for him (disguised as Telemachus himself). She would also stand at his side while the young prince conferred with the townspeople about what should be done with the suitors.

Poseidon's hatred of Odysseus is one of the main themes, and certainly the main cause of the warrior and his men being so lost in their travels. The reasons behind this begin with Poseidon's siding with the Trojans in the war, and the false offering to the god in the form of the Trojan horse. However, this would only be the beginning of the sea god's hatred of Odysseus.

Telemachus would travel by ship to visit Nestor, one of the Greek warriors in the war against Troy, often considered to be the most respectable of the Greek warriors. He then travelled to Sparta and inquired of Minelaus and Helen (who had finally returned with her husband, thus rendering the Trojan War a needless conflict over a spousal affair). They told him that his father was most recently known to have been held captive on an island by the nymph Calypso.

Now the story shifts its focus to settle on Odysseus himself. Odysseus is indeed entangled by the nymph Calypso who, having fallen in love with him, keeps him stranded on her island for the space of seven years. It's only when Hermes, intervenes that Calypso finally releases Odysseus. She gives him supplies as Odysseus builds a raft for himself.

Poseidon, still angered with Odysseus, sinks Odysseus's craft. Luckily, Odysseus had his share of allies throughout his plight, and he is obscured by the sea nymph Ino. He swims to shore, but has not only lost his craft, but his clothing as well.

He wakes on the shore, roused by the sounds of women laughing with each other. He comes out of the forest and discovers the princess Nausicaa and her maids washing their clothes in the sea. The servants flee in fear, but Odysseus beseeches Nausicaa to help him. She takes Odysseus in, giving him clothing and shelter.

While a guest of Nausicaa and the house of Scherie (the island upon which he had landed), a bard recounts two tales, one of the quarrel of Achilles and Odysseus, and the other about an affair involving Ares and Aphrodite. Odysseus, who at this point hadn't shared his identity with his hosts, asked the bard to recount the first tale. He exposes his identity by not being able to contain his emotions at the bard's words. It is from this point that Odysseus recounts his travels after the end of the Trojan War.

He began his trip home with twelve ships, carrying all of his men. They raided the city of Ismaros in Cicones. While Odysseus insisted that they leave quickly after dividing up the women and plunder, the men refused. The Cicones attacked the next morning, killing many of Odysseus's men. He and his remaining forces were able to escape, but they had their casualties.

Odysseus and his men would then come across lotus-eaters, lazy people who did nothing but eat lotus. The lotus-eaters didn't harm Odysseus or his men, but gave some of them lotuses to eat. The men who ate them no longer wanted to return home, rather, they stayed behind to gorge themselves with lotus.

Odysseus and his remaining men were then imprisoned by the Cyclops Polyphemus. Odysseus was eventually able to free himself by blinding the Cyclops, but made the mistake of telling Polyphemus his name. The Cyclops then entreated his father Poseidon (of course it had to be Poseidon).

Now filled with renewed rage toward Odysseus and his men, Poseidon put a curse upon Odysseus that he should wander the seas for the space of a decade.

Odysseus briefly came upon a hint of good fortune when they stayed with the master of the winds, a being named Aeolus. The master gave Odysseus a bag which contained the north, south and east winds. The ships came just in sight of Ithaca and everything was going well until one night while Odysseus was asleep, his men greedily opened the bag, thinking it to be treasure, and released all of the winds contained within. The resulting storm would carry the ships backward, far away from Ithaca. They found Aeolus again, but he refused to help them further.

The men set onward again, finally coming to the island of the Laestrygonians, a cannibalistic tribe. Odysseus's ship was the only one who didn't enter the harbor, and was thus the only one spared from complete destruction.

He would later run across the witch and goddess Circe. Having been warned about Circe by Hermes, Odysseus took a drug called moly which prevented what was about to happen to half of his men from happening to him. As the men ate and drank, they were turned into pigs. When Odysseus was able to resist the magic, Circe agreed to return his men to their original form provided that Odysseus would love her. They stayed on this island for a year, until Circe finally gave Odysseus the knowledge of how to contact the dead for guidance.

Odysseus traveled to an island on the western edge of the world and came across many spirits, including a crewman named Elpenor who asked Odysseus to find and bury his body. Odysseus agreed and was then visited by a prophet named Tiresias. Tiresias instructed Odysseus on how to return home without losing all of his men (not eating the sun god's flocks), and informed him that he had angered Poseidon by blinding his myopic son. He also came across Achilles, Agamemnon, Heracles, Minos, Orion, and other characters. He is eventually beset by innumerable souls from the underworld asking of news of their relatives. He retreats and leaves the island.

He returned to the island of Circe, who instructed them on the final stages of their journey. They sailed past the island of the sirens, women whose voices so entranced sailors that they steered their ships into the rocks. All of the men with the exception of Odysseus plugged their ears with bee's wax.

Next they sailed between the whirlpool Charybdis and the six-headed monster Scylla. Many of his men were lost, but Odysseus and his remaining companions made it through to safety. They would land on the island where the sun god's cattle resided. While Odysseus was asleep, all of his men chased down, slaughtered and ate the cattle. Upon their departure, the ships were wrecked, and all but Odysseus (the only one who hadn't partaken in the offense toward Helios) were killed.

He would come ashore the island of Calypso. The nymph fell quickly and deeply in love with Odysseus and forced him to remain with her until Zeus (via Hermes) demanded that he be released seven years after landing on the island; thus bringing the guests of Nausicaa up to speed.

The attendants of the party quickly agreed to help Odysseus get home. They set forth while Odysseus was sleeping and delivered him to a harbor in Ithaca where he goes on to find his own slave's quarters. Athena disguised Odysseus that he might view with anonymity the state of his house and kingdom. The slave, a swineherd named Eurnaeus, took him in and fed him.

After regaling the local farmers with a false tale about his disguised self, Odysseus comes across his own son Telemachus who had just returned from Sparta, narrowly evading an ambush by the suitors of Penelope. He discloses his identity to his son and the two set out to kill the suitors.

While in the house, being patched up, one of the maids washing his feet recognizes Odysseus's scar and runs off to tell the lady of the house. Athena intervenes, causing Penelope to be deaf to the woman's words.

Athena again intercedes by telling Penelope the following day to hold a competition where whosoever of the suitors could string Odysseus's bow and shoot an arrow through twelve axe heads could have her hand in marriage.

Odysseus joins the contest himself and is the only one capable of stringing the bow. He easily fires an arrow through the axe heads and along with his son, Athena, Eurnaeus and a cowherd he slaughters the suitors. They also hang a dozen maids who had slept with the suitors or deceived Penelope, along with a goatherd who had ridiculed Odysseus.

He finally reveals his identity to Penelope. She is at first skeptical, but when she tests him about what kind of bed they shared, he tells her accurately that it surrounds a living olive tree.

The next day, he meets with Laertes, his father, who only accepts that it's really Odysseus after the latter faithfully recounts the orchard which the former had gifted him. The story isn't quite over yet though, as the parents of the suitors set forth to take revenge on Odysseus. In her final intervention of the tale, Athena comes forth as Mentor (the disguise she had used while Telemachus was beseeching the people before his journey to Sparta) and causes them to forget their anger. Thus, the Odyssey is complete.

These large and profoundly beautiful volumes can be summed up, but hardly done justice outside of their own text. Their inclusion here is necessary, as is their inclusion in any text about Greek mythology, however, I again encourage you to read these phenomenal works for yourself.

# CHAPTER 7

*Meet Your Roman Doppelgangers*

When Rome conquered Greece, rather than abolishing the Greek's religion, they, like many groups before and after including the Christians in Rome, ascribed the existing gods of the Greeks to aspects of their own mythology.

This was particularly easy for the Romans, as the Greek religion bore many similarities to their own, in fact, had likely inspired their own. The king of the gods in Greece, Zeus, would be attributed to the Romans' god Jupiter, a god of a similar nature. Ares would become Mars, Aphrodite would become Venus, Poseidon would become Neptune, Athena would become Minerva, and the list goes on.

The reason behind absorbing the religion of the Greeks rather than replacing it outright was simple. If conquerors take over your empire and strip you of your worship, they will be met with force and rebellion. In order to secure a more thorough and a much more peaceful transfer of power, the Romans would simply assimilate the gods and myths of the Greeks into their own system of belief.

This tactic has been used by conquerors and religious groups throughout the ages, notably by Christians. Once a powerful group, and no longer quite so persecuted in Rome, the Christians adopted the pagan holidays as their own. Although Christ is said to have been born in the summer or early fall, the Christians moved the date of his birth to be celebrated on December 25th, over the Roman pagan holiday of Saturnalia and also the birthdate of the Egyptian god Horus (among many others). Likewise, the festival of Easter which is celebrated as the resurrection of Christ is based off of the spring equinox and a pagan festival of fertility (and others). The festival celebrated Ishtar, a Babylonian goddess of fertility who was killed and resurrected.

By adapting the gods of the Greeks, the Romans ensured that the people would not rebel to nearly as great an extent over their rule. In fact, the Romans tended to respect the ancient Greeks and their manner of worship, and even added solely Greek legends and myths to their own pantheon.

This was quite out of character at the time for the Roman conquerors who often demanded more than simple fealty to the emperor. The Greeks were allowed to continue practicing their religion as they had done before this time.

# CONCLUSION

Thanks again for reading this book!

It has been a long journey. From Chaos to Heracles, from the birth of the Olympian gods to the Roman adaptation of the Greek religion, the culture and mythology of the Greeks never ceases to fascinate people from all over the world.

We have read of heroes and heretics, gods and men. The tales of Greek mythology are vast and intricate, describing not only the forces of nature, but the innermost being of the Greek people, indeed, of all people in their own inventive way.

The Greek perception of death is visited by the dreaded gorgon Medusa. Life is brought forth by Prometheus. Not to mention all of the trials of Odysseus as he searches for his way home.

In learning about other cultures, we learn not only about our past, but our present as well. There is a common thread within all of us, and that can be found in the way that we relate to each other. The world is often beset by troubled times, but there is always the opportunity to come together through understanding and a commonality which runs deeper than any disagreement or perceived difference.

Whether you read this text casually or for the purpose of gaining specific knowledge of the ideas, philosophies, myths and manners of the Ancient Greeks, I certainly hope that you found in this book the object of your intention.

It has been a great pleasure to share this wonderful collection of Greek myths with you, the reader, and I hope that you will join in further reading of the other books in this series. The other books in this series include a book regarding the history of ancient Greece, along with one book each of ancient Egypt's history and mythology. I hope to meet you again through the age-old sharing of ideas that is the connection between myth and history, science and religion.

Thank you,

*Martin R. Phillips*

*A Preview of*
*Martin R. Phillips'*
*Latest Book*

# EGYPTIAN MYTHOLOGY

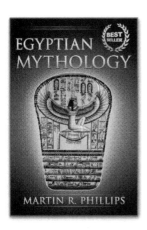

The mythology of ancient Egypt is a vast and fascinating thing to study. With up to seven-hundred gods and goddesses (and combinations thereof,) the mythology of the ancient Egyptians was complex and, like all religions thus far, would undergo changes in theory and practice over time.

There's something so compelling about the ancient Egyptians that their culture and beliefs are still popular today. Although most of the country no longer practices the religion of the ancients, figures such as Isis, Osiris, Horus and Set (to name a very few) still pop up in movies, music, art and philosophical discussion.

The mythology of the ancient Egyptians is now worldwide, and is without doubt, one of the most enduring and fascinating sets of mythos that the world has ever seen.

One of the most intriguing things about the Egyptian mythology is that there are actually a number of parallels between it and later mythologies, such as that of the Greeks, the Romans; even modern day Judaism, Christianity and Islam have many similarities with these ancient myths.

But there is that which sets the mythology of the ancient Egyptians apart. Somehow it's regal and elegant. Like many other mythologies, there are tales of good and evil, sex and violence, creation and destruction, love and loss. The phenomena of nature, humans, animals, emotions, life, love and death are contained within the vast and often inscrutable sources from which we have come to glean the meaning behind the glyphs and learn more about one of, if not the most, important cultures and mythologies the world has seen.

It's important to note that many of the Egyptian myths that we are aware of only began to be recorded during the old kingdom (approx. 2686-2181 B.C.) through use of what we now call The Pyramid Texts.

These were prayers, myths and incantations carved into the walls of the burial chambers of ancient Egypt's most important figures to ensure their safe passage to the afterlife.

The origins of Egyptian mythology are lost to antiquity; however, what we do know is more than enough to keep one busy studying for a lifetime. The pharaohs would come to be regarded as gods upon the earth, incontestable gateways between all of mankind and the realm of the gods; however, little mention of the pharaohs themselves will be made in this particular text. Here, we are primarily concerned with that which is outside the realm of governance; at least as far as it doesn't concern the religion of the ancient Egyptians.

In Egyptian mythology, we have the idea of the soul, of justice, balance, both on earth in life and after death in an afterlife... for a very short period, we even see a transition from paganism (belief in multiple gods) to monotheism (belief in one god,) although this change would not last.

The principles and morals of the ancient Egyptians are brought to life through their mythology. One of the easiest ways of understanding a people is to familiarize one's self with their beliefs, whether religious or secular, and I am very excited to take this journey with you into a realm of better understanding one of the most enigmatic societies that the world has ever known…

*PS. If you enjoyed this book, please help me out by kindly leaving a review!*

12912720R00056

Printed in Great Britain
by Amazon.co.uk, Ltd.,
Marston Gate.